Butterfly in a Bamboo Grove

FRONT COVER:
The bamboo plant and a butterfly: symbols of polar opposites and the complementarity of strength and gentility.

BACK COVER:

A giant silk cotton tree in the interior of Guyana under which I sat in the late afternoon as I contemplated the setting sun. I watched innumerable birds and butterflies as they nestled for the evening.

BIOGRAPHY

Harry Persaud was born and grew up on the West coast of Demerara, Guyana. He lived the humble life of a country boy grazing cows in open fields dreaming of colourful journeys. The West Coast was his playground where he learnt many wonderful things about nature amidst sugar cane and rice paddy fields, listening to, seeing and touching the raw pulse of life, the simple patterns which connect all things.

As a young man, he taught school on the coast and in the interior district where he was exposed to the beauty of the jungles of Guyana and the integrity and sublimity of an honest and unspoilt people of the forest. He later worked on a Sea Defence Project on the East Coast building walls.

Harry Persaud holds the Bachelor, Masters and Doctoral degrees in Anthropology having done field work in Northern India towards his Ph.D dissertation.

Dr. Persaud is currently putting together an historical recapitulation of India's cultural influences in S.E. Asia, an area he recently visited. He is also a feature writer and freelance journalist and has written articles for various journals and magazines.

Dr. Persaud is the vice-president of the Indo-Caribbean History Society of Ontario and also an organizing committee member of the South Asian Heritage Month Celebrations at the Vedic Cultural Centre in Markham, Ontario. He has published poems in Contemporary Verse From Around the World by Iliad Press in conjunction with the National Authors Registry in Michigan, having won the President's Award for Literary Excellence for a single poem.

Dr. Persaud holds a 3rd Degree Black Belt in Okinawan Karate which he taught for the past ten years at the Vedic Cultural Centre, Markham. Some of his other interests are gardening, cooking, travelling, meditating, yoga, and spending quiet moments over a cup of tea listening to soft music with his wife and sons in Toronto, Ontario.

4

Butterfly in a Bamboo Grove

Harry Persaud

Edited by Ram Jagessar
Cover design by Harry Persaud
Cover illustration by Nur Atiqah Fauzan

Toronto, Canada

DEDICATION

To my beloved mother, Maggie, who planted the seed of my thinking and nurtured its growth with deep affection. We grew flowers on rainy days to watch them bloom on sunny ones. You gave me the courage to face any situation in life and the love and compassion to share with all who crossed my path.

To my wife Shawn Marie, who has cleared many boulders in my way. I have learnt so much from you, so much more to learn. My sons Narayan and Troy, live life full, never be afraid of change.

ACKNOWLEDGEMENTS

To my many school teachers, university professors, martial arts instructors, karate students, siblings and fellow travellers, thank you for being there.

My father, for his astuteness and discipline and for allowing me to have an education.

To you my brothers and sisters of the world, we share a common destiny, your joys and pains are mine, we are of the same ancestry, our dreams and aspirations to share, our journey side by side, one breath, one heart in one Universe.

CONTENTS

INTRODUCTION	10
WHISPER IN THE WIND	13
A DROP OF WATER	15
THE FLIGHT OF INNOCENCE	17
TROPICAL SUNSET	18
THE BEGINNING	20
MY UNIVERSAL NATURE	21
MY GARDEN	24
THE HAWK HAS FLOWN	25
SPACE DUST	26
WISDOM EYE	27
DANCING LEAF	30
BOVINE BICUSPIDS	31
COCOON	32
HONEYCOMB	34
BROTHER	35
LOVE STRUCK	37
YESTERDAY	38
SILENT FLIGHT	41
MAREA DEL PORTILLO	42
WHO I AM	43
PICK A PATH	44
NORTHERN HEMISPHERE	45
FEATHERED BEAUTY	47
METAMORPHOSIS	48
LUMINOSITY	49
GENTILITY	50
LIFE	51
MINDFULNESS	52
IN THE MORNING	53
MANSION OF THE HEART	54
FIELDS OF GREEN	55
THE FLOWER AND THE BEE	57
DUST	58
CROCODILE	59
SHADOWS	60
LUSCIOUS MANGOES	61

VARANASI	63
BREATH UNFOLD	65
IF I LIVED	66
SHADOWS	68
THE FLUTE	69
TOUCH ETERNITY	70
KAMALGATA	71
CREATIVE IMPULSE	72
COMPANY	73
THE BROTHERHOOD OF MAN	75
WHAT	76
MY MENTORS	77
IN BETWEEN	79
THE STONE THAT BECAME GOD	80
INNER GURU	84
CHAKRAM	86
A DREAM	87
I WILL SEE YOU TOMORROW	89
AUGUST MOON	90
EVERYTHING	92
TRANSMIGRATION	93
A THOUGHT	96
BABY BIRD	97
INNOCENCE	99
THE COMPASSIONATE HEART	100
DREAMS	102
A RIVER OF HONEY	103
DRAGON'S TAIL	107
FOUR O'CLOCK	110
INDRANI	112
THE HAWK	115
CAYO LARGO	118
THE WHEEL OF LIFE	119
NITYA	121
THOSE WHO MUST DIE	123
LIKE THE WIND	125
REFLECTIONS ON SELF	127
ALONE	129
PARADISE	131
SUKHA	134

INTRODUCTION

Each of us has a story to tell, a poem to write, irrespective of the circumstances in our lives. Some 60,000 years ago a lonely woman knelt beside a shallow grave, placing flowers upon the body of her lost child, saying farewell to a loved one while preparing the transition of its soul into the nether world. A poet was born; there was deep affection for someone, there was beauty in the wild flowers offered and a sense of transmigration of the essence of life into a different and parallel state of existence.

Whatever the facts are, the creative imagination and the impulse for eternal life sparked the birth and growth of divinity for continuity into infinity. We were no longer mere animals, we had become humans with the propensity to understand the network of interrelatedness of all things in the Universe.

This fluidity is poetry: when birds whistle so sweetly as the sun rises, a river flows ever so gently towards the sea in search of its greater self, the sun reflecting off the face of the moon inducing gentility and love in the hearts of men and women everywhere, when thousands of 'flowered' birds dance in synchrony at breathtaking speed across mud flats never colliding, Monarch butterflies in the millions leaving Quebec and Ontario for Mexico every Autumn.

Poetry is my wife and I placing baby greenback turtles into the Caribbean Sea on their annual trip across five thousand miles of dangerous waters to find their traditional home off the coast of Africa for millions of years. Poetry is when my wife and I looked at each other with tears in our eyes wondering whether our new found friends will fulfil their perilous journey.

As humans we are also on a journey, we take a bold step forward leaving footprints upon the sands of time for others to follow, as indeed we have done ourselves following those of our predecessors. But sometimes, we must have the courage to step outside the box of secured thinking, breaking the walls of social and cultural convention and face "the land touch not" the "Neti Neti – Not This, Not That" of the ancient unmitigated enquiring mind. For therein lie vast treasures of consciousness to be discovered and shared. In the further field beyond the pale of relative reality the open mind must play to develop its creative imagination and recognize that time and space are one in a great continuum into nothingness.

As Self enfolds it creates a world in which it wants to dance, and for me this is the epitome of my journey. My poetry illustrates a timeless repose, the fluidity of change in a state of changelessness, moving forward only to go into the past, the beginning is the end, the end the beginning in an infinite circle called 'now'. The seeking of the "Suchness" without quantification or qualification of the discriminating mind crosses over into new territories.

My poem called <u>The Dragon's Tail</u> aptly describes the interrelatedness of the past to the future and the dire need to preserve both by respecting and cherishing the present. <u>Bovine Bicuspids</u> illustrates the mutual needs between plants and animals for their survival. The Zen like quiet acceptance of life's gifts in <u>Breath Unfold</u> is the sinew of one seeking calm in a turbulent sea, to fight is to lose, to embrace is Divine. In <u>A Drop of Water</u> we are never alone, we are always travelling to our larger body the ocean of truth "seeking a world beyond itself."

There is a common theme in my poetry, which is, everything blends into one another, a process of fusion and diffusion until the "dancer and the dance become One". I used the butterfly as metaphor for change from a hungry caterpillar brooding in its cocoon only to fly away as a sea of colours "hop-scotching imaginary mounds of flowers". A prime example of the human need for unity with its higher Self is expressed in the river looking for the ocean, the human aspiration to become the stars by "collapsing the world into its soul."

My passion for all that is good in life: compassion, understanding, benevolence, spirituality, are all manifestations of my collective experience both in my native Guyana and my new home, Canada. All of the wonderful people who supported me in moments of despair and laughed with me in times of joy are parts of my poetic journey, each one a key on the musical instrument of my life. I will continue to play and sing my song of love and human dignity.

WHISPER IN THE WIND

I heard whispers in the wind,

of forgotten stories of old

when times were simple and life

flowed like a mighty river

I saw visions of thought in flight

in the freedom of knowing

that boundaries are lost in the

distant horizon

I reached out to touch the skies

sticking my fingers upon

the nebulous roof of space

to draw it closer to my centre

With space came the stars and

the world,

all collapsing into my soul.

14

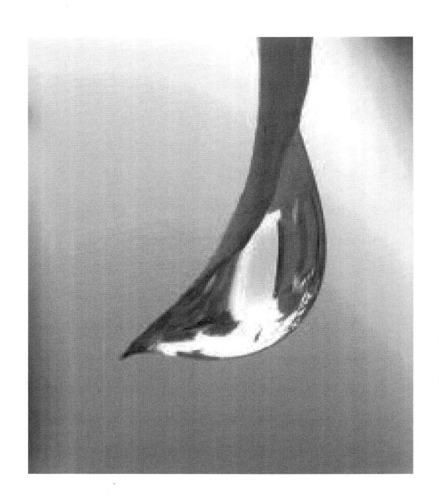

A DROP OF WATER

One drop of water falling,

falling off the edge of a leaf

into a sweet river flowing below....

...plop, the drop enters its larger body

expanding its capacity, moving

towards an unknown destination

What is this journey it has taken,

losing its singularity in the world

of the known,

now flowing into intertwined shadows

in hazy moonbeams

Silvery reflections upon translucent

fluidity flows ever gently

into a world beyond itself,

how did the stream come to be

had it not been

for innumerable droplets falling,

falling

off the edge of a leaf.

THE FLIGHT OF INNOCENCE

Tossed in the bosom of time

fluttering with colourful wings

resting upon unknown flora,

gliding, dancing, singing

moments of bliss.

A gentle touch of innocence,

a glance of love,

mutually accepting, sharing beauty

and stillness in the infinite now.

Forms and colours will come and go

but trust and understanding transcend time

for a butterfly and a little boy.

TROPICAL SUNSET

The setting sun salutes a sea of precious
colours, liquid, effervescent, harmonious;
graceful cranes like miniature sail ships
glide across the horizon bringing
to life the painted sky!

Blue-Saki, Kisskadee, Robin Red Breast
with their sweet songs like
flying Morning-Glory, golden Sun-Flower and
violet Jump-and-Kiss sing of a freedom
beyond man!

Everywhere celestial feathers blend
into terrestrial petals,
birds and flowers, song and dance
of the tropical twilight!

Humming-Birds of dynamic form,

light dancers upon sheets of velvet,

sucking nectar, fanning pollen into

thin air in an ocean of motion

without movement!

If you have not seen the majestic violet,

sapphire and crimson butterflies

like floating rainbows cutting space,

kaleidoscopic patches hop-scotching

hills and dales

If you have not experienced the crest

of the sun over the Pakaraima mountains

reflecting gold across the Rupununi Savannahs

then you do not know the glory of a

tropical sunset!

THE BEGINNING

We cannot resolve the future,

chart the map of our destination

unless we understand who we are

and from where we came.

We must return to that place and

time when our forefathers incubated

our destiny spinning the yarn which

has formulated the fabric of our lives.

MY UNIVERSAL NATURE

Everywhere I pointed

was a place of perfection

I pointed to the unfathomable skies

and there lies totality,

I pointed to the sea and there was oneness,

I pointed to a flower

and there was perfection

I pointed to the moon and there was

completion.

When my fingers turned

in the opposite direction

there was the source of Totality,

completion, Oneness,

my finger had pointed

to the centre of my heart

for in me is the source of all things...

deep space, a beautiful flower

the serene moon all manifesting

my Universal Nature

MY GARDEN

My garden looks like God splashed

a bucket of colourful paint

from heaven;

hues of azure and crimson like liquid ponds

of rainbow and golden sunshine,

scintillating

teasing the senses for more

How I wished that when I pass

from this world

to the next that the forces that be find it fitting

that I serve as a garden Deity

roaming the universe

planting seeds of flowers

opulent and abundant!

THE HAWK HAS FLOWN

A hurricane in the Caribbean

begins with the fluttering of a butterfly's wings

off the coast of Africa.

The same way

my embodiment is a shadow

cast upon the earth

by the passing

of the great universal Spirit

my mind a mere droplet in the ocean

of its presence.

SPACE DUST

And what if I lived

and became such and such

by achieving this and that,

my life will still

disappear

in the haze of time,

like space dust blowing

where once stood

a giant star.

Yesterday I was, today I am, tomorrow.....

as I remain no one

going nowhere

WISDOM EYE

I cannot be deluded into thinking that extra-intelligent forces are at work in the determination of my life's process. When we take responsibility and accountability for our actions the burdens of life are understood, often setting us free of all predeterminations. Our imagined interruptions by contrived forces shackle us into our own prison of complacency and dependency, making us servants to our delusions rather than masters of our destiny.

The wrath of ignorance

will not seal

the lid of my wisdom eye,

a wedge has been placed

to prevent closure,

once the eye has seen

no veil can avoid light

from entering

the inner sanctum

No arrogance, no false pride

to sing the song of freedom

beyond the Gods,

they wished my dance

to be of their tunes

but I do not crave their solicitations

in my moment of solitude

Who are they had it not been

for my imperfections

yet they fester upon my wounds

devouring the scabs

exposing the rawness

of my sufferings

protecting those who crawl on their bellies

towards them

Such servants are meaningless in their repose

always dependent upon

the illusory compass of ignorance

unable to see through the self inflicted

wall of dark nights

such uninitiates will not suffer

to enjoy

the sweetness of healing

Here and now my soul bathes in the sea of

aloneness

unperturbed by loneliness,

the Universe is my larger body,

the Gods my machinations

why should there be want,

I already possess everything

DANCING LEAF

.....now I see my form

dancing like a leaf

in the invisible wind,

the leaf sways its delicate

but perfect shape

to accommodate the form

of its companion,

the leaf knows not why it dances

but follows the rhythm

of that which holds it.

The same way I follow

the sweet melody

of my greater body

to take delight in its

universal song

BOVINE BICUSPIDS

.....running and dancing across meadows

singing

as gentle raindrops

run down my face on an early

summer's morning,

the crackling of bovine bicuspids snapping

yellow bells,

sweetly scented flowers disappear to reappear

as froth on the breath of a newly born calf!

Beauty nourishes life, life gives beauty in the

eternal cycle of creation and dissolution

COCOON

The tiny caterpillar does not know its destiny, it only understands that it must eat of the precious green leaves of the tamarind tree. Yet within the layers of its skin are colourful hues of yellow, red and purple sheets of velvet awaiting the morning sun to gleam from afar like miniature universes of paint splashed everywhere!

Moving colours give birth to flight ever so gently, resting upon honey suckle tasting dew drops descending from floating mists at dawn. I do not know the colour I will express in the floration of my spirituality, yet like the caterpillar I understand I must eat of the collective wisdom and knowledge before me until my soul has satisfied its hunger.

Like the caterpillar, in my ensuing sleep I will dream of celestial journeys into the nameless world where my wings will take flight bringing me to rest on the petals of forgetfulness.

When I awake from my long slumber, time and space would have disappeared leaving me no trace of the past, only new realities.

HONEYCOMB

Cultures are man made rules of conduct and values meaningful to life at specific times. I strongly believe that to hold on to the old ways for their own sake is irrational, making anyone archaic, monocausal and intolerant to new ideas. The dogmatist lacks the ability to understand separate and parallel realities, and he sees everyone outside his world view as wrong and inferior. This could be a dangerous recipe for genocide and ultimate self annihilation. Compassion is the oil which lubricates the wheel of human awareness.

I view life as a honeycomb

I suck the nectar out

and spit the wax away,

many dead habits

are chewed upon

filling the mouth with waste,

once the succulent essence is extricated,

savoured and digested

the reject should be discarded

as if never existed.

Culture is filled with wax,

but there is also honey!

BROTHER

Feel the anguish of the demise of a brother

like a burning fire deep within,

let your tears and your sufferings travel

inwards

to the centre of your Being.

In this way your tears

like a flowing river of remorse

will wash your heart centre,

the Anahata

as it travels to the soul centre

the Sahasra.

From there it will flow upwards

to connect to the world

where your sufferings will move

from passion to compassion,

from the sympathy for one

to the love for all beings

everywhere,

let your pain be your joy for humanity!

LOVE STRUCK

It's a wonderful day....

and you are the sum total of all of life,

the epitome of all potentiality,

bottled within you is eternity

broken into fragments of your shared world,

the earth, the skies, the seas and

the mountains all manifestations of

your completeness.

YESTERDAY

I realize that our ancient mentors were free of the innumerable obstacles of our modern world. As a result we now live in a much colder, sterile world lacking in love and understanding. It is when we float above the quagmire of materialistic entrapment that we ascend into freedom to develop our evolutionary potential.

Wrapped in the security blanket

of my inherited wisdom of old,

the forest of life seemed

less obscurant, less troubling

as I cut a path through the

thicket of the lower passions in life.

I felt the pangs of lust for avarice,

the tumultuous anguish

to satisfy the vermin

of my tormented flesh,

the unquenchable thirst for recognition,

the need for love from the outer world,

a cold, sterile,

dispassionate world.

But I know that above this

thick undergrowth is a canopy

of penetrating rays

creating dancing shadows

in a partnership of light and darkness.

Above the fray of it all,

a quiet sea of the still heart,

a tranquil soul

basking in the sun of realization,

the conundrums of life

have been transcended.

When we pleasure

in the dense soup of sensuality,

we remain slow drifting logs

 in a virulent sea of

self annihilation,

we will hamper the glow

in the incandescent light of

joy and beauty

SILENT FLIGHT

....be as a butterfly, friend,

rest your wings upon your

breath and gently, silently

fly to distant places

within your heart....

MAREA DEL PORTILLO

A lifetime, many lifetimes,

climbing,

slipping

falling

only to climb again,

preparing my mind and body

for a long journey within,

Alone, steadfast of resolute conviction,

a solitary soul with no name

clings to an ever changing world.

The ever crashing waves

of the Caribbean Sea

upon the curving shores

of Marea Del Portillo

remind me

of my eternity

WHO I AM

I am a silent passenger

unperturbed in time and space,

no dimension,

only a reference point,

a free flowing wave

unattached to the ocean

PICK A PATH

I stood under a banana plant

whose wide leaves

offered me protection

from the downpour.

The tapping of the raindrops

informed me

there are many realities,

I must pick one

take a bold step

towards the rising sun

peeking above the horizon

I recalled that if I picked a path

I will miss all others,

I must be free of all to become One.

One mind perishes,

one flavour, one recipe,

hunger remains still.

Nature chooses many colours,

shapes and sounds

to express her many ways

NORTHERN HEMISPHERE

The sun is over Capricorn,

the moon is over Cancer soon

she will welcome her lover

the ensuing union will create a melding

of polar opposites

bringing heart and soul together

in the Northern horizon.

FEATHERED BEAUTY

Distant waves broken against shores

reminded me of times past,

morning light,

my arrival in time and space.

Chirping atop mango tree,

head askance

the regality of feathered beauty

majestically haloed by the rising sun.

My brother the hawk

accompanied me through the night

METAMORPHOSIS

A beautiful butterfly

lit upon my shoulder

in the late afternoon

gently nesting in the nape of my neck,

its soft wings caressing

the lobe of my ear

as if it wanted to tell me its story.

It had transcended three worlds,

the world of creeping,

crawling perpetuity,

the world of metamorphosis

into a chrysalis,

of inactivity, brooding, sleeping, becoming,

only to burst into flames of colours

in a new world of flight!

LUMINOSITY

We are made from the dust

of decomposed stars

transforming

transcending in time

until we return

to that primary state

as luminous bodies

lighting the Universe.

GENTILITY

And what if I fail

to reach the top of the mountain

as long as I begin the ascent;

the attempt would set

the program in place

for transformation of mind,

body and soul.

The destination is the journey,

the sun has no occupation but to shine,

the moon no precondition but to be gentle

as it waxes beautifully.

LIFE

.....life begins

at the entry of breath

in the nostrils

and ends

at the point of departure,

life is a constant filling

and emptying.....

MINDFULNESS

What would be the stream

if my mind was not liquid,

what would be the stars

had my eyes not possess vision,

what would be sugar

had my tongue not known sweetness,

what would be the tapping of time

had my ears no hearing

what would be the illusion called reality

had my mind not dreamed of the celestial.

I am the dancer with the vision of a dance,

the ripples of the ocean

creating activity in a world of fantasy

upon which I play,

riding the crest of the wave

of my destiny

IN THE MORNING

Cool morning, salty air
 ocean splashing
whispering distant relationships
when she enveloped me
in her blanket of comfort,
placing me upon unknown shores
with her rolling fingers,
only to develop consciousness

MANSION OF THE HEART

I remember leaving one room
in the mansion of my heart
through an open door which
closed immediately behind me,
I brought many memories into this room
and I have many chambers in this house
to visit

I will return to the first room
as a refined soul,
I must not be attached
to the many things of this house
but leave them for someone else to enjoy

FIELDS OF GREEN

When my inner self wants to touch

base with me it takes the form

of a child,

it informs me of humility

of newness

and fresh wisdom.

THE FLOWER AND THE BEE

A single bee encircled,

landed upon the centre

of an ebullient perfection

fashioned by the hands of time

The ensuing fire created

a sea of honey

emanating a well spring

of unspeakable beauty

falling like tear-drops

into the souls of

lonely women everywhere,

the silent yearnings of flowers

for the touch of a honey bee!

DUST

Dust in the wind,

once a mountain in the skies

washed by clouds

flowing into river

resting on the edge of the ocean

to be walked upon

CROCODILE

hideous monstrosity

awaiting sustenance

in the dark waters of a shady lagoon,

no evil intent, no contrived fascination

with the macabre

only the need

for continuity upon the wheel of forever.

Your hapless victims become

a part of your being

their life blood flowing in your veins in the

great

play of life.

(Dark Lagoon, Cayo Largo, Cuba)

SHADOWS

The silhouette is a faint reflection

of the real,

I am but a shadow of the ultimate

a mere ripple upon the sea of time

my illusory form tells me

that there is the eternal

the solid ground upon

which I stand but do not see,

where light dissipates darkness

I am a seed awaiting germination

upon fertile soil,

I could feel the warmth of knowing,

the waters of consciousness flowing.

LUSCIOUS MANGOES

.....many moons have passed

as you grew to maturity,

many days have come and gone

as the warmth of the sun

penetrated your skin.

The moon, the sun

rising over the horizon

interlocking, dancing in the skies

nurturing you with wind,

kissing you with rain-drops

I absorb the sun, the moon

the rain through

your sticky nectar

as you become the essence

of my Being

wonderful mangoes

from the mountains of Cuba

I beseech you to fulfil

my cravings for the sacred soil

of a forgotten world

VARANASI

"Step forth" bellowed the Hindu priest
as we locked eyes in the mid-day sun
"walk through the flames" beckoning me
to walk past two sacrificial altars
on the Ghats of Mother Ganges,
 "now you leave the world of the dying
to enter the domain of the eternal,
like old clothes you will change bodies
but your soul will forever
celebrate its immortality."

"Even the Gods cannot rob you
of your divine birth-right
as you have entered
the world of the initiates,
triumphant over the fleshy nature
of the transient"

from that point on

I felt that my body and soul

had recognized they are reflections

of each other.

Life was no longer rhetorical,

it was a fusion

of knowledge with experience

in the ancient tradition of 'Om Tat Sat'

'Thou Art That'

BREATH UNFOLD

Do not ponder

over the good and

bad things of life as

karmic reward

or punishment but in quiet acceptance

live on until you are freed

of all conditions

If the air is bad or good we must still

breathe.

IF I LIVED

If I lived in the desert

I would not understand the ocean,

I could not envision

the flow of a river to its larger body.

But in the desert I will know

the vastness of space,

the innumerable grains of sand

replicating the countless stars

in the universe.

If I lived like an eagle

I would fly in the skies

to see the earth

as a blue ball in infinity,

there would be no clock, no yesterday,

no tomorrow

If I lived as a blade of grass,

I would exist without prejudice or fear

cushioning the descent of unsympathetic feet,

only to rise again

to touch the rising sun

If I lived like a fish in the sea

I would swim in its depth,

feel its fluidity,

know its unity,

its clarity,

its reflectivity

..... If I lived.....

SHADOWS

......the sun casts not

a shadow

yet it is the creator

of all shadows.

Like the sun, let your

mind be free of all

areas of darkness.....

THE FLUTE

The traveller becomes a flute

through which the music

of life is played

The melody is a beam of light

shining from the centre of the self

where there is no beginning, no end

just a journey.

TOUCH ETERNITY

Seek your inner Self, my friend

by reaching out

to your outer manifestation;

hug a tree, touch the flowing river,

feel the breeze on your skin,

see the mountain peak

silhouetting star-lit skies,

hear the whispers of inner space

telling you its eternal story,

taste dew drops in the early morning

and come to know that you are

KAMALGATA

On a Kamalgata leaf dancing at dawn

in the wind gust,

silvery dew drops move here and there

in synchrony

CREATIVE IMPULSE

I understand my intellect

and my spiritual capabilities

of taking the world in my hands

like stucco moulding

and shaping it to my heart's content.

Yesterday I was,

today I am,

tomorrow I will be

the whim and fancy of my machinations.

No cellular thinking within walls

constricting flight of thought

abundant and rife with the

creative impulse of a bee flying

from flower to flower

making honey!

COMPANY

Grace accompanies humility,

love accompanies simplicity,

truth accompanies courage,

happiness accompanies detachment,

peace accompanies understanding,

compassion accompanies wisdom,

the illumined mind accompanies knowledge.

Completion accompanies you and I

always beyond quantification.

THE BROTHERHOOD OF MAN

I envision a world without war, racial prejudice and hunger. My song is, we should all live in harmony and peace, cherishing our unique status as humans. Petty differences are as ripples upon the sea of life which are not the product of the sea itself but the results of extraneous circumstances interrupting the placidity of the ocean. We must not allow ripples to become tidal waves ripping us apart.

Many rivers a common source

radiating fan-like across

plains and mountains

Rivers of many colours flowing

endlessly to the sea.

Black, brown, white and yellow waters

mixing, filtering their impurities

but remain one

Soon all will be crystal clear,

purity will sparkle as reflected sunbeams

on morning dew

All shall be one and one shall be many,

times will be when consumed minds

like meandering streams

cut new paths to the estuary of truth

the eternal sea of humanity

WHAT

what is beyond the horizon

that is not within

my mind's eyes,

what is so sweet in sugar

that is not within

my tongue,

what can I touch and feel

that is not

already within me!

MY MENTORS

The Earth is my mother,
she has given me birth
and sustenance nurturing
my precious blood with
life giving energy

The sun is my father,
he melted the clouds
allowing the essence of rain
to germinate my form,
giving me identity

The moon is my friend,
she beckons me to follow,
in her gentle way
filling me with compassion

I acknowledge my body

made of mother Earth,

my heart embodies the Sun,

my soul the moon!

IN BETWEEN

I stood on a fine line

leading from this world to another,

one foot in the world of causation

the other in my heart centre!

I am dancing on the head of a

white cobra caught between

the finite and the eternal

THE STONE THAT BECAME GOD

Everything turns to face the sun,

even the rock

at the base of a shallow river,

wishing to feel the sun's warmth

to experience its light,

awakening lethargic sleeping energy

from deep within.

In time it will be transformed,

decomposed,

dying to be reborn

becoming soil which washes

upon an unknown shore,

feeding the trees of its sweetness

expressing its desires of reaching the sun

through the limbs and the leaves

to become beautiful flowers and

delicious fruits

which feed the bees and the birds

making honey,

taking flights into fields afar.

This is how the unmoved moves,

the inorganic becomes organic

in the great leap of life,

the simple becomes the complex

in the great play of time.

All things reflect one another

on the great journey of unity.

Life is meaningless in separation

so the lion must eat the lamb

the lamb must eat the grass

which lives off the stone

that became soil.

The soil feeds the trees

to bear flowers and fruits

for the bees and birds

which must transcend

by offering food to humanity.

Humans then develop thoughts

to create Gods

to further their flight

into the great Cosmic dimension,

creation of the Gods created by humans;

a field of frivolous frolicking

upon which humans ponder

and the Gods play.

The flowers and its fruits

being the heart and soul

of the Celestial,

the dream of the Stone

to create a world of Oneness,

boundless and timeless

establishing the reality

of the rock in the water

rolling along gently on its way

to becoming a God.

INNER GURU

While our senses are as rough waters

you are that quiet

but deep stream

unfathomable in your silent wisdom

CHAKRAM

I merely strive and function

from the fourth chakra,

the heart centre,

from this centre

we exercise compassion

for all beings.

Here the Buddha's hands meet

bringing Earth and Sky

together in the middle way

A DREAM

A dream, no more real than the wake
of a bird long gone to its nest
in the hills yon high!

A dream no more real than the flame
that was and the smoke that floats
in the sky!

A dream, no more real than
yesterday's memory nor
tomorrow's hope!

A dream, no more real than
a butterfly's attempt to hop-scotch
imaginary mounds of flowers!

A dream, like silken dew-drops
which vanish with the rising sun!

A dream, you enter my life like a fantasy conjuring up in me illusions of the past, a dream!

I WILL SEE YOU TOMORROW

I arrived from the East

following the setting sun

as I travel through time,

here I will rest for the evening of my life,

in the morning I will awake to a new dawn

only to follow the dance of my soul

to catch another glimpse of eternity

AUGUST MOON

In the silence of the August moon

I emptied my mind of its plenitude

no shadow cast upon it

no reflection created by it.

I could hear the falling leaves outside

my window, the fluttering wings of

butterflies settling in the early evening

the whispers of lovers in embrace,

the cries of warriors in battle in far off places.

I could hear my heartbeat

like resounding echoes of distant drums

in synchrony with the rhythm of the Universe.

I could not see you but my mind

has encased your form

dancing in a silhouette

in the tropical full moon

You beckoned my soul

to follow in the wake

of your terrestrial journey,

tasting, seeing, hearing,

touching your presence

always aware of your stillness

in the centre of my being.

EVERYTHING

Do not for one moment doubt

your inner Being,

already in essence

you are everything,

open the gate and let the water

of Self-hood flow,

my friend.

TRANSMIGRATION

We accept the reality of transmutation but we must also entertain the possibility that the finer energy of Self could accompany its grosser manifestation through time. To be human is to know that we know, to develop complex emotions such as love and compassion, to watch the setting sun with awe and fascination. The Doe did not know of its impending transcendence into humanity but because of its gentility was given the responsibility of being human, it had entered into another level of realization.

Fleet-footed doe

travelling with the speed

of the wind across Savannah

skipping air twenty feet at a time,

breath leaving lungs

as if a sledge hammer

pounded against its chest.

Its heart ached

as it pumped gallons of blood

The doe's feet hardly touched

the blades of yellow grass

resembling the golden manes

of its pursuers,

they scented its blood

as it left a trail
of red upon yellow,

they came from everywhere

undaunted by its speed and its altitude

It was cut off at a gully

near a water hole,

felt the sharp fangs

of an azure-eyed king of the beasts

draining its lifeblood

breaking bones,

devouring flesh,

tearing its heart from a

fragile chest

In their carnivorous orgy

the doe became one

with its golden-maned nemeses,

torn heart was freed

as it watched the spectacle below

In death it was reborn

void of the limits of time and space

the silver cord of attachment to Terra firms

now in the entrails of its predators

basking in the sun

The doe liked the world of light,

the ground was prepared for its return,

the reward for past peaceful existence,

the beginning of its journey into humanity

A THOUGHT

A thought travelled to the corners

of the universe and returned with

a message that infinity

has been reached.

BABY BIRD

Fallen from heights sublime,

neither of earth nor sky

you await the sound

of love and sustenance.

In the early morning

as the sun warmed your bodies

love flew off

delightfully singing a song

as old as time

With tender wings

You try to fly to distant lands

only to fall upon the rocks below

On that torrid day

crawling upon dirt

you found each other

embracing eternally

as your souls took flight

into the nether world

to dance amidst the clouds.

The cries of love can be heard

into the still dark night

(mother bird returned at dusk to feed her

lost babies)

INNOCENCE

...the incense stick burns slowly

exuding the exotic aroma of spirituality

similarly my heart burns releasing

its passion for the world

and compassion for all life...

THE COMPASSIONATE HEART

Wrapped in the centre of the heart of humanity, I feel its pulse, its pains and pleasures, I could dance with its rhythm like a silvery dew-drop rolling here and there on a silky eddoe leaf. I felt that this transition of consciousness illuminated my mind to observe the great play of Lila but also to be absorbed into the workings of the Universal Mind, where as a tiny ripple I merge into its sea of compassion, melting as a grain of sugar in a pot of honey.

I was no longer looking for meanings on the outside since all reality emanates from the centre of my Being. But the final reality in this world of the heart is not mine to claim, it belongs to no one. There is a single heart beating in the Universe from which we have all taken portions off, some more some less, yet is abundant and free. It escapes those who misuse it and those who wish to own it, it becomes like the wind in the open hand which rushes out once the fist begins to tighten around it.

The open heart is the compassionate heart, it is a huge reservoir of patience and love. The compassionate heart seeks nothing yet it offers everything, it requires neither recognition nor approbation. It is a place where there is eternal peace and beauty.

DREAMS

What you sow as a young man

you will reap as experience

when you are older,

so dream dreams of fruits abundant

in the garden of youth

so that the fields of manhood

be rich in the crops of Self hood

A RIVER OF HONEY

Taking her final transition in life,

my mother handed me her heart

in the form of a glass of milk

and a rice cake

after we had planted flowers all day.

We enjoyed nurturing the plants,

that was where our hearts were,

during planting we hugged many times,

that was when I felt

she was transferring her heart to me.

I realized after her passing

several hours later she gave me

the greatest gift in my life;

a benevolent heart, a wonderful heart!

which is why when I experience

intense joy or sorrow

she appears in my dreams,

reminding me as to who I am.

I do not hold on to this treasure

but everyday I gave it away

and the more I give away,

the more it seems to multiply my capacity.

I now understand that

tilling the soil,

adding plant food,

tying back limbs to fence,

fetching water,

cutting branches,

picking flowers

were to prepare me for life.

Each action a symbol

of creating the condition,

nurturing and enjoying

the fruits of my labour.

The being which is heart-centered

will run smoothly whatever the terrain,

all experiences at this level are

Self fulfilling.

At the upper levels of the heart centre

the shadows of the past disappear,

time is no longer linear;

the perfume of a flower,

the sparkle of a star,

the passing of a loved one,

the sorrow of the world,

dew-drops glistening on a moon-lit leaf

all co-exist in a moment of time.

In a centred heart

 the beginning is the end,

the end the beginning

in an infinite circle of completion.

The world had become

a river of honey!

DRAGON'S TAIL

The dragon eats its tail.

It has gone full circle,

it cannot spit fire

since it has burnt the field

upon which it once roamed.

No new souls to convert

no new territory to conquer

no known horizon to guide its sail

to the far land

Where can it fly in this eleventh hour,

did the dragon not envision that the

present is determined by the past,

the future moulded by the present?

In the infinite circle the head is the tail

this the dragon knows but not why

time is circular,

the past and the future,

are the present

stretched backward and forward.

The dragon does not understand this,

it will self-annihilate

since its head, the present,

will go into its past to burn its tail

the future,

that which balances its being

There is a lesson to be learnt in humanity.

Should we destroy the future

with the flames of the present

so that we never have a past again?

Should the fragrant flowers be gone,

the sweet songs of birds be distant echoes

in the dark vacuum of nevereverness,

a sleeping dragon for perpetuity?

I see a dark cloud on the horizon.

FOUR O'CLOCK

You glanced at me

amidst mango leaves

at four o'clock,

like a love sick calf

I waited and scanned the horizon

every day at four o'clock,

As you appeared my heart flew

to reach the skies,

your smile of compassion

all I could see

from my lofty recluse

at four o'clock

A world of ecstasy

the ocean of love

your eyes beckoned me

to their depth of placidity

Dear mother I await for four o'clock

INDRANI

Large brown eyes set deep

in chocolate coloured face,

thin arms and legs dangling

 a maimed and grotesque body

as if Indrani was a caricature

of nature's rejected inventory

Hungry, thirsty and cold

in a lonely world

lacking dignity and humanity

a solitary soul looks for sustenance

Indrani, what beguiling force

has made you its prey

to trash amidst the shadows of avarice

on life's desolate journey

My heart cries in agony

when you look up and see

merciless eyes

reflecting callous intemperances

uncaring, unsharing

of its ill-begotten wealth

as you grope for protection

under the canopy of the skies

Indrani, your soul

is not different from mine

it strives for perfection

like a wilted flower

amidst the slugs of inhumanity

constantly stepped upon by soulless harlots

Indrani my sister, the moment of truth

would have dawned upon us all

when you nor I no longer

shed a tear for each other,

when we have forgotten

how to be humans.

(In honour of a little homeless girl in Varanasi, India)

THE HAWK

"A hawk has flown over your head", said an Ojibwa Elder to me as we crossed paths in an open field at a powwow in Winnipeg, Manitoba

......the hawk chose space as its habitat, fathomless with the capacity of accommodating all possibility. With a single leap into the sky the the hawk encircled the halo of the sun indicating that the large is small and what is far is near; when we feel the heat of the sun, we are touching it, when we breathe in air we are ingesting space, when we quench our thirst, we take in the ocean. The many stars are our fragmented consciousness; everything we perceive we become, we are the light in the fire; the salinity in salt; the sweetness in sugar; the fragrance of a flower; the silence before the din of the birth of the universe. We are the tumultuous roar of the lion, the fury of a hurricane, the powerful crashing of waves on a shoreline. We are dew-drops rolling off velvety petals, we express ourselves as the thunder in the skies, the song of the canary transferring into the soft wings of crimson butterflies gently stroking kamalgata lilies. We are the thought which became the Universe, the moon which waxes and wanes in the skies as the sun departs until tomorrow. When I am in Sahasra, what is there to know, to be, to do that is not already in bloom in the garden of my soul. I can only walk through, seeing, touching, tasting knowing that I am.

The hawk was me in full radiance to discover my true self as I travel non-chalantly, timelessly in a domain of freedom. The hawk understands this freedom as it flies in a circle always returning to the beginning, seeing the invisible line in space following the path of energy left behind, returning again to that place which is everywhere, it is everything yet nothing.

What do I do, where do I go from here? Nowhere, I am already there, I am able to loosen the knots of delusion spun by the dream Master as he creates his web of deception. The truth is untenable and can only be experienced and not told. With the speed of thought the hawk disappeared on the horizon as if never existed. I felt its wings fluttering in my heart, its talons clutching my soul for another journey.

CAYO LARGO

I have seen the blue sky

touch the silvery ocean

and in their moment

of deep fusion

I was lifted

by a crest of the lovers' fury

only to lay spent

upon the shores

of contentment

(Cayo Largo, Cuba)

THE WHEEL OF LIFE

The wheel of life

will not roll smoothly

on a rocky road,

a jolt here and there

awakens the traveller

on his journey

preventing further illusions

of the sleeping mind.

The arduous task

of climbing and falling

must be met

with the unyielding desire

to continue.

There are many cool

and refreshing brooks

on the road side

which will temporarily

satisfy your thirst

but you must not fall asleep

my sons,

on the path to freedom

NITYA

I saw the fingers

of the sun as it climbed

over the horizon

Love sprung forth

as a ball of flames,

setting ablaze the

hearts and souls of

all in its presence!

THOSE WHO MUST DIE

They stood firm upon forbidden ground

shedding their blood,

listening to the wail

of their women and children

Their agony heard long into the night

as they painfully tend

the festering wounds

of their fallen comrades

No land, no home they have,

a history of tears and hunger

a life of constant flight

into illusion

Their souls hurry along

to a world free of exploding shells

and crumbling buildings,

they belonged to the Earth,

once lived in the valley below

the laughter of their children

haunting shadows of lost memories

Their fore-fathers lived, loved and

died among a yellow sea of sand,

of figs and frolic amidst palm fringed

oases of a once peaceful land

On a still night broken by howls

of jackals, the young poet sings

his dreams of brotherhood,

now his ghost weeps as it reflects

upon a world of carnage and insanity.

LIKE THE WIND

Give me strength

like the wind

to fly to distant places

to touch many faces

like the wind

let me climb hills

never standing still

free of all ills

like the wind

making waves

forming clouds

free of movement

like the wind playing music

dancing through

meadows swaying

forms and shadows

as I kiss

earth and sky

like the wind

let me fly

REFLECTIONS ON SELF

I think righteous and act well

when I reflect upon you,

like the expanding universe

my mind embraces

your transient form

Like a grain of sugar

your sweetness

provokes my senses

invoking my need

for more

Like soft music

your presence

enchants my mind,

at the arrival of dawn

you brighten my world

At twilight you depart

with grace

ALONE

There was a gentle mist

falling from the skies

moistening the soft petals

of a beautiful flower

swaying alone

in the August moon!

PARADISE

I ran through fields
of dampen earth of
emerald green foliage
of palms and meadows

My heart was gladdened
as the setting sun
displayed a sea of colours
across the horizon, gleaming
like a precious jewel around
the neck of the world

My mind danced with the
flowing wind
kissing falling leaves
cushioning their descent
to the earth

Soon the rising moon
beckoned me to her
bosom of love, soft and
sumptuous in her delight
her succulent rays bathed
my body with peacefulness

Little candle flies lit
my path with their
fluorescent explosions
as pungent aroma
of ripe mangoes saturated
the calm evening

The swaying shadows
of coconut palms imitated
living forms on the
ground as I moved
in synchrony with their
abandoned freedom

The throbbing in my heart
echoed in my mind a message
that must be told,
beneath the tropical skies
life blooms with a nostalgic
fervour more intense than the
passion of the Gods

SUKHA

Gentle mists,

sun at Dawn

as flowers bloom

with rolling dew-drops

upon petals,

butterflies dancing

signalling all is

well!

Made in the USA
Charleston, SC
19 April 2011